N I C K   F A W

Unwrapping the seasons All-age talks for Advent and Christmas

Kevin Mayhew

First published in 2001 by
KEVIN MAYHEW LTD
Buxhall, Stowmarket, Suffolk, IP14 3BW
Email: info@kevinmayhewltd.com

The material in this book first appeared in *Getting It Across.*

9 8 7 6 5 4 3 2 1 0

ISBN 1 84003 788 1
Catalogue Number 1500453

Front cover design by Jonathan Stroulger
Illustrations by Graham Johnstone
Typesetting by Richard Weaver
Printed and bound in Great Britain

Contents

Introduction

I will never forget the day at Bristol College when I received the orders of service prior to my first preaching engagement and saw leaping out at me two words: Children's Talk. Clearly this was viewed as an integral part of the service, but what exactly was expected of me, still less how I could deliver it, I had no idea. My experience in talking to children was, to say the least, limited, and there was little I had learned up to that point which had prepared me for the task. Had I but known it, no formal training was to be offered in this field anyway, the learning process essentially consisting of being thrown in at the deep end.

I squirm with embarrassment when I look back on some of the early 'children's talks' I delivered, the content simplistic if not downright patronising. Numerous congregations must have exercised enormous patience as slowly I developed my technique at their expense. Yet, strangely, the person who taught me more about the art of successful communication than anyone else was not a member of any one of these congregations, nor one of my college tutors, but an elocutionist I saw for a few brief sessions during my time at Bristol College. His advice consisted of three simple tips:

- always begin by asking a question or using an illustration which involves your audience in what you are saying;
- always end with a simple challenge or question which puts in a nutshell everything you have been trying to say;
- keep the middle short, simple and to the point.

In every address I have given since then I have kept that advice in mind, not following it slavishly but attempting to apply the essential principles whenever possible. They have stood me in good stead. While I have never considered myself a particularly gifted preacher, still less a natural communicator, the talks I have given throughout my ministry seem generally to have been well received. Why? Partly perhaps because my sermons were always short, but most of all, I believe, because listeners could always find something to relate to.

Having said that, every talk is different. The style of a sermon is quite unlike that of a lecture – at least it should be! The style of a wedding address is nothing like that of a funeral oration. Similarly, the style of a children's talk – or family talk, as I prefer to call it – is totally different again. When young people are present in church you are immediately talking to a wide age-range, spanning two, three or even four generations. It is essential not to talk down to children, and equally important that adults get something more from the talk than a pleasant sense of indulgence. This is all the more important if my suspicion is correct that many adults actually prefer listening to a family-type talk than a sermon, the latter often pitched so far over their heads that their thoughts soon wander to such matters as the state of their Sunday lunch or yesterday's football results!

So what makes a successful family talk? There is no one answer to that, but for me the following are all vital ingredients:

- an element of fun
- appropriate visual aids
- 'audience' participation
- all-age relevance
- brief applications
- thorough preparation
- attractive presentation

Let me deal with each of these in turn.

Fun

With any audience a little light-heartedness goes a long way towards establishing a rapport. When talking to young people this becomes all the more essential, as there are so many other attractions in our society competing for their time. Too often I have attended services in which the 'talk to the children' is little more than a mini (or not so mini) sermon, and the ineffectiveness of this approach has been eloquently testified to by scarcely suppressed expressions of boredom. Not only do such talks fail to get the message across but, far worse, they effectively drive young people away from our churches.

Visual Aids

My own preference has always been to include some sort of visual aid in a talk, even if this is simply key words stuck to a board. Indeed, words and words games, as you will see, figure prominently throughout this book. It is a fact that what we see stays in our minds far longer than what we simply hear.

Audience Participation

Young people (and many older ones too) like to be involved in a 'learning process' rather than simply being talked to. Games, wordsearches, quizzes and other such forms of participation offer an effective way of including the congregation in what you are saying. We need to promote an atmosphere in which people feel part of what is going on.

All-age Relevance

As I have said already, many adults are actually far more receptive to a talk geared towards a younger audience than they are to a sermon.

Many also enjoy participation as much as children, if not more so! Even if this were not the case, we owe it to any congregation to ensure that a talk is able both to stimulate and challenge.

Brief Applications

I have always believed that the secret of a successful family talk is to keep the application – the serious bit at the end – as short and simple as possible. Ideally, the message you are looking to put across (and this ought to be *one* message, not several) should speak for itself through the illustrations and visual aids you use, though some expansion of what this means is usually necessary. Overdo the application and you will pay the price. Which of us hasn't witnessed the sudden glazed looks the moment the 'religious' part of a talk is reached. Whatever you do, don't try and ram the point home; if you haven't made the point through the fun part of your talk, you won't make it afterwards.

Thorough Preparation

There is no getting away from it: talking to young people takes time. There were many occasions during my ministry when I spent longer preparing a single family talk (even one lasting a mere five minutes) than two full-length sermons. In this book I have attempted to do most of the spadework for you through suggesting ideas and ways of presenting these, but to deliver most of the talks you will still need to spend some time in preparation. Don't be put off by this. The effort may occasionally seem out of proportion to the time taken up by the talk during the service, but I believe the results will more than justify it. What you put in, you will get out.

Attractive Presentation

In this sophisticated age, young people as much as adults are used to slick, glossy and professional presentations. While we cannot emulate these, it is important for visual material to be as clear and well presented as possible. The advent of the home computer makes this far easier to achieve than it once was, as well as saving huge amounts of time. While material can be written out by hand (for many of these talks I did just that), I would strongly recommend the use of a PC word-processing package if possible.

When it comes to displaying material, my own preference, arrived at after several years of trial and error, is to use a magnetic whiteboard in conjunction with magnetic tape (available through most office stationery suppliers), with the back-up of a second whiteboard (magnetic or otherwise) and Blu-Tack. You will also need easels for these, as light and portable as possible. A supply of thick coloured marker pens (in washable and permanent ink) is a must for many talks, as is a copious supply of thin card and/or paper. Several of the talks could be delivered using an overhead projector and screen if this is preferred to board and easel. Adapt to your available resources.

On a purely practical note, make use of a radio microphone if this is available. Family talks often involve a degree of movement, and it is all too easy to stray from a standing microphone so that you become inaudible, or, worse still, to trip headlong over the wires of a halter neck model! (The younger members of the congregation will delight in this, but for you it can prove embarrassing and even dangerous.)

Each talk in this collection is set out according to a basic framework:
- a suggested Bible passage which should normally be read publicly prior to the talk
- a statement of the aim of the talk
- details of preparation needed beforehand
- the talk itself.

This last section includes instructions relating, for example, to the use of illustrations, together with a suggested application of the talk. The talks will work best if, having read and digested these paragraphs, you present them in your own words. This is particularly true where the congregation is invited to respond, and developing and incorporating their ideas and answers into the talk will require a measure of ad-libbing on your part.

Each of the talks in this booklet have been used in public worship during my time in the ministry. No doubt many are flawed in places and could be considerably improved – I do not offer them as examples of how it should be done, but rather as a resource which may be of help to you. Of all the comments received during my ministry, few have gratified me more than those when young people have referred in conversation to talks I delivered three, four, even five years back. Whether they remembered the point I had been making I cannot say, but whatever else they had enjoyed being in church and carried away positive associations of their time there. That in itself was always sufficient motivation to spend further time and energy devoted to getting the message across.

Nick Fawcett

ADVENT

1   Hope

Reading   Matthew 1:21-23

Aim   To explore the key theme of Advent – hope!

Preparation   In large letters print the following riddle:

My first is in HIDDEN but not found in SEEN.
My second's in COMING but not there in BEEN.
My third's in PROMISE and also EXPECTANT.
My last is in EASTER as well as in ADVENT.
My whole is a word that can mean many things,
from confident trusting to wishful thinking.

Display this in a prominent position from the start of the service.

Talk   Invite the congregation to solve the riddle – some may already have done so. The answer, of course, is HOPE. Run through the riddle again for the benefit of those who haven't solved it, showing how this answer is reached.

Hope is one of the loveliest words in the English language, and something we all need to have in life. So perhaps that is why Advent is such a special time for so many – for it is all about hope: hope that one day Christ will come again and establish his kingdom.

As in the riddle, the truth of that promise is HIDDEN to many, rather than SEEN. Yet, trusting in what has BEEN, we are confident Christ is COMING again. We have that PROMISE from Christ himself, and this season reminds us always to be EXPECTANT, for we do not know when that time will be.

Advent is a time full of HOPE – not just vague WISHFUL THINKING but CONFIDENT TRUSTING in the Christ who shall come again!

2   Keywords for Advent

Reading   A selection of short readings are used as part of this talk (see below).

Aim   To emphasise the serious message of Advent.

Preparation   Print the following in large letters on strips of card and stick them to a board:

> ???? YOU WERE HERE
> ???? DANCING
> DON'T ???? UP
> GREAT ???????????
> ?????, STEADY, COOK!
> THE ?????? OF SHERLOCK HOLMES
> TALES OF THE ??????????
> ????????, SURPRISE
> ?????DOG
> ????? WITH MOTHER

Print off the words in bold under **Talk** below, and retain these for use as required.

Talk   Display the board and invite the congregation to suggest the missing words. You will need participation from older members of the congregation, since many of the answers won't mean much to the children. Insert the missing words over the question marks using a piece of blutack, as follows:

> **WISH** YOU WERE HERE
> **COME** DANCING
> DON'T **WAIT** UP
> GREAT **EXPECTATIONS**
> **READY**, STEADY, COOK!
> THE **RETURN** OF SHERLOCK HOLMES
> TALES OF THE **UNEXPECTED**
> **SURPRISE**, SURPRISE
> **WATCH**DOG
> **WATCH** WITH MOTHER

The names of films, books or television programmes provide us with keywords for Advent, each reminding us what this season is all about.

From early in their history, the Jewish nation held on to the WISH that the promised Messiah would COME. Across the centuries they learned to WAIT patiently for his coming, although sometimes they found it hard to curb their EXPECTATIONS. Yet when Jesus finally came they were not READY to receive him.

Advent warns us against doing the same. It calls us to be ready for the RETURN of Christ whenever that might be.

So Matthew tells us:

You must be ready because the Son of Man will COME at an UNEXPECTED hour . . . *(Matthew 24:44)*

Or as Paul's first letter to the Thessalonians puts it:

This day should not SURPRISE you! *(1 Thessalonians 5:4)*

Again we read, this time from the Gospel of Mark:

What I say to you I say to everyone: 'WATCH!' *(Mark 13:37)*

And finally, from the Gospel of Matthew:

Keep WATCH, because you do not know the day or the hour . . . *(Matthew 25:13)*

Advent is a special time which looks forward to Christmas, but it is also a time with a message of its own – a message we cannot afford to ignore.

3   A book of books

Reading   2 Timothy 3:12-17

Aim   To show that the Bible is not one book written about 'religion' at a certain place and time, but a collection of living stories, written over thousands of years, and reflecting the needs and situations of countless people – a book which is challenging to read, but rewarding for those who persevere.

Preparation   Print off the following on strips of card:

> DOMESDAY
> LIBRARY
> HYMN
> NOTE
> TEXT
> HAND
> GUIDE
> PRAYER
> EXERCISE

Attach these to a board and display at the front of the church.

Talk   Show the congregation the words above, and ask what single word could be placed after each of them. The answer, of course, is BOOK. Explain that these are just some of the many books they might read or use during the course of an average week. Invite them to guess from the clues below the names of other types of book they might read.

1. A special sort of book published once each year.
   (Annual)

2. A book used for checking the meaning or spelling of words.
   (Dictionary)

3. A book for listing items, or for mail order.
   (Catalogue)

4. A book you may need if you want to ring somebody.
   (Telephone directory)

5. A book for looking up information.
   (Encyclopedia)

6. A book full of maps covering the whole world.
   (Atlas)

7. A book used for planning ahead, or for recording past, present and future events.
   (Diary)

8. A book for storing things like photos, stamps and cards.
   (*Album*)

9. An instruction book.
   (*Manual*)

10. A book used for looking up Bible verses.
    (*Concordance*)

11. A book you might use to find words of the same or a similar meaning.
    (*Thesaurus*)

12. The name sometimes given to a personal organiser.
    (*Filofax*)

13. A book used to write down music.
    (*Score*)

14. The book through which we believe God speaks to us.
    (*Bible*)

These are examples of all kinds of books written for all kinds of purposes by all kinds of people, and in a sense that is exactly what we find in the Bible, for it is not just one book but a whole collection. Some are about history, others hymns and songs; some are full of proverbs, others of words spoken by the prophets; some are letters, others stories about Jesus; some are about the future, others about the past. Though we call it *the* Bible, it is not *one* book but *sixty-six*, each of them different, reflecting different situations, different needs, different times! That is why there is always something more to learn and new to discover within its pages, and that is why this collection of books speaks to so many people in so many ways.

But there is one thing that binds all the books of the Bible together, and we can see what that is in Paul's second letter to Timothy:

> As for you, continue in what you have learned and firmly believed, knowing from whom you learned it, and how from childhood you have known the sacred writings that are able to instruct you for salvation through faith in Christ Jesus. All scripture is inspired by God and is useful for teaching, for reproof, for correction and for training in righteousness, so that everyone who belongs to God may be proficient, equipped for every good work.
> (*2 Timothy 3:14-17*)

The Bible is not always an easy book to read. We need help and guidance to understand it. But if we make time to study what it has to say, we will discover words which give meaning to all of life!

4   Expecting

Reading Matthew 24:36-44

Aim To bring home the fact that Advent is not an excuse for speculating about end times, but rather an opportunity to prepare ourselves for the unexpected return of Christ.

Preparation You will need two alarm clocks (one with a loud bell, if possible), a flash gun or camera with built-in flash, two balloons (one inflated), a sharp pin and an empty bucket. Before the service set one of the alarm clocks to go off at the beginning of your talk – this will need some pretty fine judgement on your part!

Talk Tell the congregation that you are going to test their ability to predict the future. Keep talking on this theme – for example, ask them how good they are at predicting the weather or football results – until the alarm you have pre-set goes off. Ask how many expected that! Reset both clocks, one to go off in two minutes and one in three, and then, keeping the clock faces turned away from the congregation, ask them to predict which will go off first. When one eventually goes off, ask who picked the right one. In the meantime pick up the flash-gun/camera, and ask what will happen if you press the 'control button' (demonstrate). Pick up an inflated balloon and a pin, and ask what will happen if the two come into contact (demonstrate!). Blow up the other balloon, then ask what will happen if you let go (demonstrate!). Finally, pick up the empty bucket, pretending it is full of water. Ask the congregation how many of them will get a soaking if you throw it over them (demonstrate, and enjoy the consternation giving way to relieved laughter!).

In all of these situations, there was a fair chance of predicting what might happen, and in some it was possible to predict precisely. There are some things, though, we can't foretell. For example, will there be a white Christmas this year? Who will win the next World Cup? What numbers will come up on the Lottery this week? Such questions are almost impossible to answer with any certainty, despite the attempts of many to try.

The same thing is true when it comes to Advent – a season for looking forward, anticipating the future, preparing ourselves for the coming again of Jesus Christ. The reason we light our Advent candles is to symbolise our mood of expectation at this time.

When, though, will he come? The answer is we do not know, we cannot know, and we do not need to know. As Jesus told his disciples:

> About that day and hour, no one knows, neither the angels of heaven, nor the Son, but only the Father. Therefore you also must

be ready, for the Son of Man is coming at an unexpected hour. *(Matthew 24:36, 44)*

It is not *when* Jesus comes that matters, but the fact he *will* come, in God's own time. There is no point in speculating about times and places; such things are unimportant. What matters is that we live in such a way that, whenever he comes, we are happy to be found by him, and ready to welcome him as our living Lord and Saviour.

5   Books of the Bible

Reading   2 Timothy 3:14-4:5

Aim   To get across the message that God speaks through the Bible – and that we need to read it!

   (This talk is suitable for any Sunday of the year, but is especially suited for Bible Sunday.)

Preparation   On large pieces of paper or card reproduce the following 'Catch-phrase' clues.

Ruth

Hosea

Acts

Exodus

Timothy

Amos

Judges

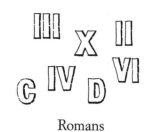

Romans

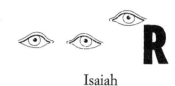

Numbers

Isaiah

A STITCH IN TIME
SAVES NINE
TOO MANY COOKS
SPOIL THE BROTH

Proverbs

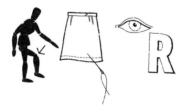

Lamentations

Nehemiah

Esther

F EE BOTHAM
ST JOHN

WRIGHT
McCASKELL

Ephesians

1 Peter

Song of Songs

Nahum

**CHARLES I
HENRY VIII**

2 Kings

Micah

Personalise this picture so that it
resembles your own car by putting in your
number plate, colour, you driving, etc.

You will also need to prepare a sheet with the answers, which you can reveal one at a time, making sure that the bold letters line up vertically, as shown below, so that the message can be read. (On the right-hand side are explanations of the answers which you may like to use to give clues where necessary.)

RUTH	(Roof)
HOS**EA**	(Hose, ear)
ACTS	(Romeo and Juliet)
EXO**D**US	(Exit)
TIMOTHY	(T, moth, E)
A**MO**S	(**A** rolling stone gathers no **moss**)
JUDGES	(Judges)
ROMANS	(Roman numerals)
NUM**B**ERS	(Numbers)
IS**A**IAH	(Eyes, eye, R)
PROVER**B**S	(A stitch in time, etc.)
LAMENTATIONS	(Crying)
NEH**E**MIAH	(Knee, hem, eye, R)
ES**T**HER	(S, stir)
EP**H**ESIANS	(F, Es, Ians)
1 PET**E**R	(1p, eater)
SONG **OF** SONGS	(Singing)
NAH**U**M	(Neigh, hum)
2 KIN**G**S	(Two kings)
M**I**CAH	(My car)

Talk   Begin by asking the congregation how many books there are in the Bible (66), how many in the Old Testament (39), and how many in the New Testament (27). Explain that you have chosen twenty books for them to identify from your 'Catchphrase' drawings.

When all the answers have been revealed, explain that there is a serious message in all this and ask if anyone has spotted it – 'Read your Bible through'.

These are just some of the books of the Bible, but, as we were reminded earlier, there are 66 books in all. How many of these could they name? And, more important, how many have they read?

Reading the Bible isn't always easy, especially some of the lesser-known books in it, and there will be times, as with the clues above, when we spend time wondering just what a particular passage means. We need help, advice and support if we are to get the most out of our Bibles. As Christians, though, we believe the Bible is a record not only of the way God has spoken to his people in times past, but his word to us now; a book which has a message for everybody and every part of our lives; a book which opens the way to knowing God and living life as he wants us to live it.

It's true that the Bible can be hard to understand, but if we make time to study it we will find the effort more than worth it, for we will discover God speaking his word to us!

6 A time to prepare

Readings

Isaiah 40:1-5; Mark 1:1-13; Luke 1:8-7:2

Aim

To bring home the fact that Advent is a time of preparation, not just for Christmas but for the final return of Jesus Christ.

Preparation

Print in large, bold type the letters in the following wordsearch:

	1	2	3	4	5	6	7	8	9	10	11	12	13	14
1	A	L	O	C	U	S	T	S	D	N	H	O	J	R
2	S	S	E	N	E	V	I	G	R	O	F	V	L	E
3	H	E	I	S	A	I	A	H	N	Y	A	W	L	P
4	O	R	E	T	A	W	T	B	B	E	L	T	I	E
5	L	T	H	O	N	E	Y	A	Y	O	J	A	H	N
6	Y	R	T	D	R	O	L	P	S	N	I	S	E	T
7	S	E	H	A	I	R	I	T	M	E	E	L	L	A
8	P	S	T	N	O	S	O	I	J	C	E	E	I	N
9	I	E	P	W	I	N	E	S	E	I	V	V	J	C
10	R	D	N	R	U	T	R	E	S	O	O	E	A	E
11	I	E	Y	D	A	E	R	D	U	V	D	L	H	P
12	T	J	O	R	D	A	N	A	S	R	L	O	W	E

Attach magnetic tape to the back of each letter and arrange them on a magnetic board exactly as above. (You may find it helpful to draw in the lines of the grid using a washable marker pen.)

Talk

Explain that you have prepared a quiz based on the three passages read earlier, together with a wordsearch on which can be found the answer to each of the questions. Ask the following questions one by one, and see if anybody can spot the appropriate word or words on the wordsearch. Remove them letter by letter from the board. The answer and its location in the wordsearch are given after each question.

1. Who were the two New Testament readings about?
   JOHN (top row, reversed)

2. What two things are we told John ate?
   LOCUSTS (top row, across) and HONEY (row 5, across)

3. What were John's clothes made from?
   HAIR (row 7, across)

4. What did John wear around his waist?
   BELT (row 4, across)

5. What didn't John drink?
   WINE (row 9, across)

6. Where did John preach?
   DESERT (column 2, up)

7. What was Zechariah told John's birth would bring to him?
   JOY (row 5, reversed)

8. Which prophet foretold John's coming?
   ISAIAH (row 3, across)

9. What was God's messenger sent to prepare?
   WAY (row 3, reversed)

10. What did Isaiah say the rough ground would become?
    LEVEL (column 12, up or down!)

11. What would every mountain be made?
    LOW (bottom row, across)

12. What every other thing would be made low?
    HILL (column 13, up)

13. What did Isaiah say would be heard in the desert?
    VOICE (column 10, up)

14. Whose glory did Isaiah say would be revealed? The glory of the . . .
    LORD (row 6, reversed)

15. In whose spirit and power did John come?
    ELIJAH (column 13, down)

16. What did John do to Jesus and the people?
    BAPTISED (column 8, down)

17. In which river did John baptise?
    JORDAN (bottom row, across)

18. What did John baptise with?
    WATER (row 4, reversed)

19. What did he say Jesus would baptise with?
    HOLY SPIRIT (column 1, down)

20. What did people have to show before being baptised?
    REPENTANCE (last column, down)

21. What does repentance mean?
    TURN (row 10, reversed)

22. What did this repentance lead to?
    FORGIVENESS (row 2, reversed) of SINS (row 6, reversed)

23. What descended on Jesus after John baptised him?
    DOVE (column 11, up)

24. What did God call Jesus after his Baptism?
    SON (row 8, reversed)

25. What was John sent to make the people?
    READY (row 11, reversed)

26. For whom did John make the people ready?
    JESUS (column 9, down)

The display board should now read as follows:

A							D				
										V	
	E						N				
					T						
										A	
		T									
					I		M	E			
		T			O						
		P									
					R						
	E										P
						A	R				E

The remaining letters spell out a message: Advent – a time to prepare.

This one phrase summarises all the words we have picked out from the wordsearch, for Advent is, above all, a time for preparing, for ensuring we are ready to celebrate the coming of Christ and to welcome him when he finally comes again. It is the need to prepare for the coming of the Messiah which Isaiah was talking about, which John the Baptist preached about, and which this season is all about.

Isaiah spoke of God's messenger who would prepare the way for the promised Messiah. John came to prepare that way, making it clear what people needed to do if they were to be ready for his coming, and today challenges us in turn to ask whether we are ready for his return.

Advent is not simply a countdown to Christmas; it is a God-given time to prepare ourselves to receive Christ, to receive the forgiveness and new life he brings, and to commit ourselves afresh to his service. Have we made time to prepare?

CHRISTMAS

7 The heart of Christmas

Reading Luke 2:1-7

Aim To show that unless Jesus is at the heart of our Christmas celebrations, we will fail to understand what this time is all about.

Preparation Print the following combinations of letters on to small pieces of card: SA, AUS, R, F, DE, ONS, MI, ES, TU, Y, T, EL, WR, PER, C, OLS, ST, NG, CR, RS, PR, TS. Attach magnetic tape to the back of each, and place on a magnetic whiteboard as follows:

SA   AUS
RU   F
DE   ONS
MI   ES
TU   Y
T   EL
WR   PER
C OLS
ST   NG
CR   RS
PR   TS

Then print these combinations: NTA CL, UDOL, CORATI, NCE PI, RKE, INS, APPING PA, AR, OCKI, ACKE, ESEN.

Again, stick magnetic tape to the back of each piece of card, but keep these separate, ready to stick on the board during the talk.

Finally, print the following: CHRIST, CHRIST, CHRIST, WHITE, MAS, FATHER, MAS, HAPPY, MAS.

Again attach magnetic tape and keep separate for later use.

Talk Show the congregation the combinations of letters you have arranged on the board, and ask if they can make sense of them? Offer the clue that they are all to do with Christmas. Invite suggestions, and fill in the missing letters as each correct answer is given, as follows:

SANTA CLAUS
RUDOLF
DECORATIONS
MINCE PIES
TURKEY
TINSEL
WRAPPING PAPER
CAROLS
STOCKING
CRACKERS
PRESENTS

All of these words are familiar terms associated with Christmas, but when we take the centre out of them suddenly they no longer make sense. The same is true with the following, only this time it's much easier to spot what's missing?

WHITE	MAS
FATHER	MAS
HAPPY	MAS

The missing word, of course, is CHRIST. And just as 'Christ' here makes sense of these letters, so Christ also makes sense of this time of year. Unless we have Christ at the centre of our Christmas it really doesn't make sense, for there will always be the most vital part missing.

We may enjoy all these other things we have talked about, for they are all a part of our Christmas celebrations; but we will not discover the happiness and the joy God wants us to discover if Christ is missing.

It is only when we put Christ at the heart of Christmas that we will understand what this time really means.

8 The message of Christmas

Reading Luke 2:8-20

Aim To remind us that, in all the fun and celebration of Christmas, there is the special message of God's coming to us in Christ.

Preparation Print the following words in large letters on separate strips of card:

PUDDING
CAROL
SHOPPING
CARD
DAY
PARTY
STOCKING
TREE
FATHER
EVE
PRESENTS
CRACKER
WHITE
BONUS
DECORATIONS
FAYRE
DINNER
CAKE
CACTI
WRAPPING PAPER
LIGHTS

Attach magnetic tape to the back of each piece of card.

Talk Tell the congregation you have prepared a festive quiz for them. Explain that all the answers have 'Christmas' in them, and all they have to do is supply the missing word from the clues you give them. Read the following clues, and after each correct answer, stick the appropriate piece of card on a magnetic board, ensuring you position each one precisely as shown above.

1. Something we eat after Christmas turkey?

2. Songs we sing at Christmas?

3. Buying in food and presents for Christmas?

4. Something we send to our friends?

5. Comes after Christmas Eve?

6. A special festive occasion we might enjoy at work, school, or home?

7. Something we hang up before going to bed on Christmas Eve?

8. Something we bring into the house and cover in lights and decorations?

9. Someone who comes down the chimney bringing presents?

10. Comes before Christmas Day?

11. Things we give to family and friends?

12. Something we pull at Christmas?

13. What we call Christmas when it snows?

14. Extra pay we may be lucky enough to receive at Christmas?

15. Things we hang on trees or round rooms and shops?

16. A fund-raising event we may hold at church?

17. What we tuck into as part of our celebrations?

18. Something else we may eat at Christmas?

19. A plant that flowers around Christmas time?

20. Something we use to cover our presents before we give them?

21. Something we put on the Christmas tree, or which we might see in a town centre?

All these things together go to make up our celebration of Christmas; all kinds of things which we will be enjoying over this season; and there is no reason why we shouldn't have a good time and enjoy them all. Yet, are they finally what Christmas is about? The answer, of course, is no, but there is a danger if we focus on them too much that they may hide the true message of Christmas. In fact, they have done just that here. Ask if anyone has spotted the true message of Christmas hidden within the answers – 'Glory to the new-born king'.

These are words we sing in the great carol *Hark, the herald-angels sing*, and words which take us to the heart of Christmas – not presents or turkey or cards or pudding, special though all these may be, but the birth of Jesus Christ, the Son of God, the one who reveals the glory of God and shows his love for the world.

9 Where is he?

Reading Matthew 2:1-11

Aim To demonstrate that Christmas isn't simply about celebrating the coming of Jesus long ago, but more importantly about our personal response to him, now.

Preparation Fold in half eight A4 pieces of stiff paper to make A5 cards. On the front of these write the following words in bold letters:

JUDEA
BETHLEHEM
MANGER
STABLE
HOUSE
NAZARETH
JERUSALEM
EGYPT

On the inside of each card, again in bold letters, write 'NOT HERE!' Place the cards prominently around the front of the church so that the word on the front of each can be seen.

Also prepare eight pieces of A4 paper with one of the following written in large, bold letters: E, I, H, H, S, R, E, E.

You will also need a question mark sign and an exclamation mark sign.

Talk Ask the congregation if anyone can remember what the wise men asked Herod when they came to Jerusalem? (Where is the one born King of the Jews?) Explain that you want to ask this question again today, and that to do so you need eight helpers. Invite volunteers to come to the front, and pin one of the single letters (E, I, H, H, S, R, E, E) on the front of each.

Invite each volunteer in turn to look behind one of the cards to discover where 'the King of the Jews' has been born. After each unsuccessful attempt ask the volunteer to display the words inside – NOT HERE! – and to stand at the front of the church until all eight volunteers are standing side by side in a line.

Observe that, despite the volunteers' help, your question remains unanswered. Ask the congregation to look again very carefully, and see whether they might have missed something. Allow time for people to think, then line the volunteers up so that the letters pinned to their fronts spell 'HE IS HERE'.

That's the answer to our question. Or is it? Well, not quite, for it all depends on what comes after these words. (Position yourself at the end of the line.) Is it a question mark (hold up '?'), or is it an exclamation mark (hold up '!')?

We all know Jesus was born in Bethlehem of Judea; we all know he was born in a stable and laid in a manger because there was no room in the inn; we all know his parents came from Nazareth, and that they took Jesus later to Jerusalem; and we probably know that after Jesus' birth they fled to Egypt to escape Herod.

All that is part of the wonderful Christmas story we know and love so well, but unless there's another chapter in that story, then all the rest doesn't finally mean anything. It is only when Jesus can also be found here in our hearts, in our lives, in each one of us, that Christmas truly comes alive.

Where is the one born King of the Jews? Is he simply here (point to one of the cards), or here (point to one of the volunteers), or here (point to the congregation)? Or can we point to ourselves and say, honestly and without hesitation, 'He is here!'

That's the question we need to ask this Christmas, and the answer we need to give.

10   God with us!

Readings	Isaiah 9:2-6; Matthew 1:18-25

Aim

To show that Christmas is as much about us today as those who were present in Bethlehem on the night Jesus was born.

Preparation

Cut out pictures from old Christmas cards, books and magazines to illustrate the following: Bethlehem, angel, manger, night-time, three kings, inn, shepherds, angels, stable. Avoid any picture which specifically shows Jesus as a baby or child. Place the pictures in prominent positions around the church.

Write or print the following on strips of card in large capital letters:

O LITTLE TOWN OF BETHLEHEM
THE ANGEL GABRIEL FROM HEAVEN CAME
AWAY IN A MANGER
BORN IN THE NIGHT
WE THREE KINGS FROM ORIENT ARE
NO ROOM FOR THE SAVIOUR IN BETHLEHEM'S INN
WHILE SHEPHERDS WATCHED
ANGELS FROM THE REALMS OF GLORY
CHRIST IS BORN WITHIN A STABLE
UNTO US A BOY IS BORN

Fix these to a board or the wall at the front of the church.

Talk

Tell the congregation you have prepared a Christmas quiz for them, based on the words of the Christmas carols displayed at the front of the church. Invite volunteers to come forward and match one of the pictures to one of the carols.

At the end of this exercise there should be the first line of one carol left on its own with no picture to match, *Unto us a boy is born.*

We have found pictures which illustrate each of the carols except this last one, and there's a good reason, for Christmas is not only about Bethlehem, the stable, Mary, the wise men and shepherds, but about us! That is what the reading from Matthew tells us:

The virgin will be with child and will give birth to a son, and they will call him Immanuel – which means, 'God with us'.
(Matthew 2:23)

Today we look back to the very first Christmas, and to what God did in Bethlehem nearly two thousand years ago, but we also celebrate *this* Christmas, and what God has done, and is doing, for *us*, here and now!

For to us a child is born, to us a son is given, and the government will be on his shoulders. And he will be called Wonderful Counsellor, Mighty God, Everlasting Father, Prince of Peace . . .
(Isaiah 9:6)

That is the truth we celebrate today – Jesus has been born for us. So if we want a picture to illustrate this carol, let's stop when we get home and look in the mirror. And, when we do that, let's ask ourselves two more questions: Have we understood what Christmas is all about? And, if so, have we accepted the gift God has given us in Christ?

WEEK AFTER CHRISTMAS

11 God's house

Reading Luke 2:41-52

Aim To show that while the place in which we worship is only a building, it can also rightly be called 'the house of God'.

Preparation No preparation is needed for this talk, unless you want to add to the list of questions suggested.

Talk Tell the congregation that you have prepared a quiz about houses. All they have to do is tell you who lives in each of the places you are going to mention. Invite responses.

- Who would you hope to meet in 10 Downing Street? *(The Prime Minister)*
- Who would you hope to meet in Buckingham Palace *(The Queen)*
- Who would you hope to meet in Lambeth Palace? *(The Archbishop of Canterbury)*
- Who would you hope to meet in the Vatican? *(The Pope)*
- Who would you hope to meet in the White House? *(The President of the United States)*
- Who would you hope to meet in 11 Downing Street? *(The Chancellor of the Exchequer)*
- Who would you hope to meet in Highgrove House? *(Prince Charles)*

Although many of these places are not these people's real or only homes, they can nonetheless be found in these places at some time during the year.

Now ask whom we hope to meet in church? (God.) Ask whose house Jesus told his parents he had been in when they returned to Jerusalem to find him sitting in the Temple. (His Father's house.)

While God isn't limited to any one place or time, and although the Church is more about people than bricks and mortar, a church building is a special place where we come to focus our thoughts on God; a place set apart where we recognise his presence, where we speak to him and where we worship him. That is why we call our church building 'the house of God' – a place where we can come and meet *our* Father, and enjoy his presence.

12   After Christmas

Reading   Matthew 2:1-12

Aim   To bring home the truth that though the Christmas season may be short, the Christmas message goes on being as relevant afterwards as ever.

Preparation   Using computer graphics, pictures from Christmas cards, drawings by Sunday School children, or your own artwork, compile a tableau Christmas scene, featuring Mary, Joseph, Jesus in the manger, shepherds, cows, donkeys, star, etc., but not the wise men. Display this at the front of the church.

You will also need some props which are 'leftovers' from Christmas – a deflated balloon, a pulled cracker, a discarded piece of wrapping paper, for example.

Talk   Begin by asking the congregation questions such as: How many 'days' of Christmas are there? How many of you are still celebrating? What sort of Christmas did you have?

After all the build-up, Christmas is over all too soon, and for many each year it seems to be a bit of a let-down; like a deflated balloon, a pulled cracker, or a discarded piece of wrapping paper (show your examples). Yet, while Christmas itself is over, what it celebrates is not finished! Point to the tableau you have prepared, and ask the congregation what's missing. When they spot that the wise men aren't there, ask them if they have any idea why not.

Although we think of the wise men as an essential part of the Christmas story, it is almost certain that they arrived in Bethlehem some time after the birth of Jesus, well after the shepherds had been and gone. There must have been times on their long journey when they wondered whether, when they finally made it to their destination, it would be too late, the event they had come to see long over and done with.

Yet, although what we might call the first Christmas was over when they eventually arrived, the truth behind it, and the reason we continue to celebrate this festival, was as real then as ever! Jesus had been born in Bethlehem – the King of the Jews, the Saviour of the world – and so they fell down and worshipped him and celebrated. No doubt, those few moments with Jesus must have lived with them for the rest of their lives.

So it is for us today. Christmas may be over, but our worship and thanksgiving continues; for the truth we have celebrated goes on being as meaningful and relevant today, tomorrow and every day. God has come among us in Jesus, he has shared our humanity, he has opened up the way to life, he is by our side through his Holy Spirit, and he will go on being with us for all eternity. Thanks be to God!

NEW YEAR AND EPIPHANY

13   A new start

Readings

Ezekiel 36:26-28; 2 Corinthians 5:17

Aim

To illustrate that, no matter how many mistakes we make, God always gives us the opportunity to begin again with a clean slate.

Preparation

Prepare an eye-catching poster advertising your church, or one of the activities within it. Include several glaring mistakes! Display in a prominent position.

Talk

Ask if anyone can spot the deliberate mistakes on your poster. Ask what people normally do if they make a mistake while writing something – for example, a Christmas card, a school essay, a letter to a friend, an important document. Look for answers such as: rub it out; Tippex it out; cross it out; write over it; stick something over it; start again. Apply each suggestion to a part of the poster.

There are many ways we can try and rectify a mistake, but usually they don't produce a very good result. Try as we might we can't quite disguise the fact that a mistake has been made, unless, of course, we give up and start again. Once we go wrong, it is very hard to put something right.

If that's true with something as simple as writing a letter or a card, it's all the more so with life in general. So many of the mistakes we make can live with us for the rest of our lives. One error of judgement, one thoughtless action, and not only do our own lives end up in a mess, but those of the people around us. No matter how hard we try to put it right, so often the damage is done. At best we may disguise it, but it is hard, if not impossible, to remove the scars altogether.

How often in life wouldn't we like the opportunity to start afresh; to tear out our blotted copybook and begin again with a clean sheet? We'd like nothing more, but surely that's impossible? Well, many will say it is, that there's no way we can put the clock back, but in the Bible we read a different story. Nowhere more so than in those wonderful verses from today's readings:

A new heart I will give you, and a new spirit I will put within you; and I will remove from your body the heart of stone and give you a heart of flesh. I will put my spirit within you, and make you follow my statutes and be careful to observe my ordinances. Then you shall live in the land that I gave to your ancestors; and you shall be my people, and I will be your God. *(Ezekiel 36:26-28)*

So if anyone is in Christ, there is a new creation: everything old has passed away; see, everything has become new! *(2 Corinthians 5:17)*

These words take us to the heart of the Gospel, offering good news to all. Whatever our mistakes, however we may have failed, whoever we may be, God is always willing through Jesus to offer us a new start! Not only that, but he works to change us deep within, so that next time the challenge comes we will not make the same mistake again.

We all fail sometimes, we all go wrong more than we'd like to admit, but, no matter how many times we let him down, if we seek God's forgiveness and ask for his guidance, he is ready to wipe the slate clean and help us start afresh!

14   The God who holds the future

Reading   Jeremiah 29:10-14

Aim   To show that we can leave the future safely in God's hands, confident that he will never fail us.

Preparation   On strips of card print the following words in large, bold characters and fasten magnetic tape to the back of each.

JANUARY brings the	SNOW
FEBRUARY brings the	RAIN
MARCH brings	BREEZES LOUD AND SHRILL
APRIL brings the	PRIMROSE SWEET
MAY brings	FLOCKS OF PRETTY LAMBS
JUNE brings	TULIPS, LILIES, ROSES
Hot JULY brings	COOLING SHOWERS
AUGUST brings the	SHEAVES of CORN
Warm SEPTEMBER brings the	FRUIT
Fresh OCTOBER brings the	PHEASANT
Dull NOVEMBER brings the	BLAST
Chill DECEMBER brings the	SLEET

Arrange those in the left-hand column in order down the centre of a magnetic white board. Fix the words from the right-hand column alongside the months in random order, ensuring that none fit together – for example, Dull NOVEMBER brings the PRIMROSE SWEET; JANUARY brings the TULIPS, LILIES, ROSES.

Finally, print and attach magnetic tape to the following, and display these randomly at the base of the board, keeping a mental note of the correct chronological order.

NEW YEAR'S DAY
VALENTINE'S DAY
MOTHERING SUNDAY
EASTER
FA CUP FINAL
MIDSUMMER'S DAY
WIMBLEDON
SCHOOL HOLIDAYS
HARVEST FESTIVAL
HALLOWE'EN
GUY FAWKES NIGHT
CHRISTMAS

In this last group you will need to check in which month Easter falls, and insert another event for April if necessary.

Talk   Tell the congregation that, since it is the start of the new year, you have prepared a quiz which looks forward to some of the things which the coming year will bring. Their job is to sort out the lines of a famous poem about the months of the year. Read out the lines as they stand, and ask how each one should read. Put the correct endings with each line until the whole reads as above.

Without comment at this stage, move to the second part of the quiz, and ask if anyone can match the list of events at the bottom of the board with the months of the year. Position these on the left of the board.

There are some things in life, as in the list of events above, which we can predict with complete certainty, each of them scheduled to take place at a certain time and on a certain date. Others, however, are not so guaranteed, even though we might sometimes like to think they are. Take, for example, those lines we completed earlier. Here is the poem they were taken from:

> January brings the snow,
> makes the toes and fingers glow.
>
> February brings the rain,
> thaws the frozen ponds again.
>
> March brings breezes loud and shrill,
> stirs the dancing daffodil.
>
> April brings the primrose sweet,
> scatters daisies at our feet.
>
> May brings flocks of pretty lambs,
> skipping by their fleecy dams.
>
> June brings tulips, lilies, roses;
> fills the children's hands with posies.
>
> Hot July brings cooling showers,
> strawberries and gilly-flowers.
>
> August brings the sheaves of corn,
> then the harvest home is borne.
>
> Warm September brings the fruit,
> sportsmen then begin to shoot.
>
> Fresh October brings the pheasant,
> then to gather nuts is pleasant.
>
> Dull November brings the blast,
> then the leaves are falling fast.
>
> Chill December brings the sleet,
> blazing fire and Christmas treat.

These words supposedly sum up the things we might expect to see during the course of a year. Yet, how true are they? Does it always snow in January, or rain in July? Is November always dull, February always wet, and March always windy? It may often be, but in this country, as every weather forecaster will tell you, we can never be certain from one day to the next, let alone one year! If that's true of the weather, it's even more so with most of the other things in our lives. Much as we'd sometimes like to know what the future holds, still more be able to plan it the way we want it to be, the fact is that we can't. We have to take one day at a time, and make the best of every moment.

Yet that doesn't mean the future is uncertain, because at the heart of our faith is the confidence that God holds the future of everyone and everything in his hands. Though we may not know what tomorrow may bring, *he* does; his love always watching over us, his hand always ready to guide. As the prophet Jeremiah put it long ago:

> Surely I know the plans I have for you, says the Lord, plans for your welfare and not for harm, to give a future with hope.
> *(Jeremiah 29:11)*

These words are as true for us today as when they were first spoken. If we are ready to put our trust in God, he has a purpose for us, so that whatever the future may bring, we know that God will be with us in it. We come, then, today at the beginning of a new year; a time full of promise and expectation, for making plans and looking ahead, though perhaps also for some a time which brings anxiety as they look ahead to an uncertain future. Whichever we are, we can put our faith in God, and our hand in his – he will not let us down.

Finish with the hymn *I know who holds the future* (Youth Praise).

15   News for today

Readings   Isaiah 52:7-10; Mark 1:1

Aim   To show that, though the news of the birth of Jesus is, in a sense, 'old news', it goes on being Good News for today, as relevant, as exciting and as important now as when it was first announced.

Preparation   Collect a selection of headlines taken from local, national, church and Christian newspapers (one from each paper). If possible, get hold of some regional newspapers from outside your area, and select headlines linked to that region. Make sure that all the papers you use are at least a day old. Cut out the headlines, and display them around the front of the church. Print or write, on separate strips of card, the names of the papers you have used, together with the date of the headline. Display these on a board, one underneath the other. You will need Blu-Tack or magnetic tape for this, and also for later in the talk. Finally, open a large Bible at the beginning of Mark's Gospel, and display this at the front of the church.

Talk   Read out the various headlines displayed around the church, then point to the names of newspapers and corresponding dates displayed on the board. Invite volunteers to come and select a headline and match it with one of the newspapers. If they get it right, stick the headline next to the name of the paper. If they get it wrong, ask the congregation where they think it should go. Persevere until you get the right answer.

Explain that all of these headlines were, not so long ago, items of news, whether locally, nationally or internationally; but now they are old news, no longer of much interest to anyone except those perhaps who specialise in archives. Old news soon becomes 'old hat'.

Or does it? For there is one more news headline sitting here at the front of the church which we've missed. Ask if anyone can spot it and give them a moment to consider. The 'headline' you are looking for is Mark chapter one, verse one. Pick up the Bible and read from this: The beginning of the Gospel of Jesus Christ . . .

In these words we have news which is way, way older than any of the headlines we looked at a moment ago, but it is unlike any other news, for it is still as much news today as it ever was. Why? Because Jesus was born not just for people then but for us today, and though he died, he rose again and is alive here and now. Here is news not just for a few but for everyone; not just for others but for us all! It is news which will go on challenging, inspiring and moving people day after day, from now through to eternity: Good News which will remain Good News until the end of time!